MAPPING THE MOOR

MAPPING THE MOOR

Keith Howden

PENNILESS PRESS PUBLICATIONS

www.pennilesspress.co.uk

Published by

Penniless Press Publications 2019

ISBN 978-1-913144-02-9

Cover image: Keith Howden

CONTENTS

Mapping the Moor   7

Familiar Landscapes   18

Team Photographs   23

Seven lost Chapels   41

Neighbours   48

Runes   49

A Language for Stones   51

Long Causeway   52

A Saltways Catechism   54

Whitsun   56

Cracked Mary's Mill   58

Barley Top   61

Mapping the Moor

(for my Father, 1904 -1993)

1.

Maps draw their makers' minds,
chart the spirit's orreries to display
a different ghost. Under the land's
icon lies another geography.

My father's father's Lancashire,
my father's, mine records a sour
religion sucking austere
sustenance from the famine moor.

We knew a barren contour
of tight lips. Our maps sanction
no legend for the ardent or
lexicon for his death's occasion.

2.

On his old maps, curlews
named moorland over soot Maydays
in mill villages. Delirious,
arching to a remembered cause,

he shouted, *'Where's the accident?'*
No tracks invade that region
or charts presume that continent.
How do you tell a dying man

he is the accident? Precise
cartographies of the real
encode within their geographies
a shuddering spiritual.

On my new maps, Mercedes
commuters tart mill cottages
in the moor. Geographies
unchanged wear shifted images.

3.

I mean our maps. A map dances
its maker's mind, sings somewhere
within its graphic assurances,
the spatial fables of another

and ineffable territory.
He said, *'I'm not much use at dying,
I've never done it before.'* In my
museum of charts, I hang

that ultimate cartography
of flesh's dependency, the bleak
boundaries of eternity
encompassed in a stale joke.

4.

A blackened psalm-box heaving
harmonium bleaknesses
and hymnal caterwauling
into my moor wrangles its place

on all our maps. Within its cramp
marshalling yard, the menhir
regiments and the sooted pomp
of grocers' obelisks require

reveille's bugle where the fell's
bleak code and barren signature
ethic the self-denials
implicit in our contour.

And once, in sudden sunlight,
during alchemies of sleet,
I saw its prison railings bright
as a necklace of marcasite.

My father's father's Lancashire,
my father's, mine, records a sour
contagion mapping austere
apocrypha on our famine moor.

We sanctified a parable
of tight lips. Our maps' custom
denied a lexicon or scale
or language for love's idiom.

I mean a map. My map dances
its maker's mind, incarnate, rants
within its graphic assurances,
fables attempting sustenance.

5.

I mean a map. But how translate
the heart to flattened landscape?
This was a quarry grief and that
some outcrop pain. Can any map

encompass and hold retrievable
in paper correlatives,
the feint, uncopiable
lattices whose grid contrives

labyrinths in dimensions
that have no northings, eastings,
the transubstantiating zones
of the mind's rememberings?

I mean a map more than cartoon
similes and simulation.
But by what logarithm can
the heart's countries be known?

How make a chart so integral
that, subliminal, it maps
the making of itself, and all
shifting allegiances and shapes

lie esemplastic in its scheme?
I mean maps: lost parables
of barren farms, forgotten intake's
apocrypha, that sour religion's

anathema. I mean a map
whose arcane undertaking
is parthenogenesis, whose trope
the guile of its own making.

6.

It is my map, but how to say
his dying moved me? Not the death
but the self's seismology
metamorphic within its myth.

My father's father's Lancashire,
my father's, mine, nurtured the sour
osmotic autisms that were
the instinct language of our moor.

We traded barren contours
of tight lips. Our maps deny
the ostentation of remorse,
the luxuries of threnody.

I scrawl a map above a map.
He said, *'I'm not much use at dying,
I've never done it before.'* This shape
I scheme on cellophane to bring

another map beneath and see,
by lineage or the chance
of duplicate geography,
an imposed equivalence.

'Why are they always,' she said,
such hostile landscapes?' She meant,
skirting the moor, the crowded
fables under us, the immanent

apostasies of the past.
I draw that map. The parables
of spent workings: the manifest
of ruins: the runes of broken walls.

And sometimes, jewelled sunlight
transmuting a thunder rain
has conjured dearth's palatinate
to the landscapes of Cockaigne.

7.

On his old maps, curlews
named moorland over lost Maydays
in mill villages. Mine pursues
a shifting weather's ironies.

I make a map of time, one wry
and existential second stilled.
In it, on flat-cap holiday,
charabanc mashers are held

in equipoise, soot calyxes
of blossom seize in an opulent
embalming. Memory fixes
that howl of *'Where's the accident?'*

where simian, in oriental
attitudes of carved bone,
caged monkeys, for gawp's festival,
are staring tarsier from stone.

Fermata strangles the band's
tuba kazoo. Spring's anthem
of larks in the moor's hinterlands
is hushed. In sunlight's stratagem,

the swingboat's stayed pelota,
straining at counterpoise,
preserves the stilled parabola
of its compliant prejudice

with death. Somebody's Woodbine
droops unlit. Somewhere a silent
palaver boils and someone
is shouting *'Where's the accident?'*

A boat upturned farts sucker-cup
in the mill lodge's frame. Lost oars
skulk crocodile. On the bank slope,
a keyboard of drowned flesh infers

that bright day's gothic havoc.
Then larks rage unfrozen. The swingboat
remembers its plunging arc.
The monkeys scratch their fleas. That shout

encodes its semiotic shriek
in a prism hiatus
where being resumes its antic
and clockwork nothingness.

On my new maps, Mercedes
commuters are tarting barns
in the mill villages. The past's screes
weather to capital's religions.

I chart an ironic anguish,
a map less to mean than be,
whose metaphor stalks language
for its implicit geology.

8.

It is my map. Secret in my
chartroom's hangings, there is
that Chapel's long apostasy
carved in the soft integrities

of a living cell. Etched in
a dying mind's integument
is that Mayday mayhem: someone
is shouting, *'Where's the accident?'*

Deeply scrimshawed into bone
are landscapes of spent industries,
rank farms, the failing benison
of lime in intake's bitterness.

'Why, always for you,' she said,
'are they hostile landscapes?' She meant
the moor's immanence, the crowded
apocrypha of its taint.

The marshalled menhirs of a yard
necklaced in iron wait display.
Obelisk alleys are scored
intaglio on a dry eye.

We traded in a religion
of tight lips and knew no chart
for subtler exploration
of the geographies of the heart.

I mean a map whose contours
flex esemplastic, yoking
compacted doctrines to enforce
the textures of its own making.

I mean a map. My map stutters
its maker's mind, lisps somewhere
within its coded structures,
its apprehension of a queer

and more arcane peninsula.
He said, *'I'm not much use at dying.
I've never done it before.'* In a
museum of joke charts, I hang

that ineffable region
of flesh's state, the wry acrostic
of nowhere, dry-point within
my doubting dialectic.

Familiar Landscapes

1.

Familiar landscape, the embattled road
beleaguered on the fell, climbing in coils
towards emplacement barns at broken guard
on the moor's famine marches. Dry walls,

the breastworks of attrition frontiers,
straddle on hostile ridges where spike wire
arches to shield decrepit pastures,
barbs a disputed border with the moor.

Bleak-mile-post farms keep sentry, sit
in camouflage, observing warily
from limed and levelled fields, the retreat
of civil cultures in a territory

where moats of marsh and slime concede
the moor mobilising, massing its squads
of ling and gorse. Larks' enfilade
rifles each sector and in caltrop fields

rushes are marshalled for guerrilla war.
This land was never yours. No truce will quell
the propaganda rumble of the moor
relentlessly at broadcast. Every subtle

fraternisation is a treachery.
The token force is weakened by erosion
where attrition favours those who lie
thickest and know the landscape. Occupation,

fortification and an alien culture
rudely enforced, will not outlast a slow,
rebellion resentment. And you are
foreigners here. The lark's bullet says so.

2.

Under slack pylon cables, the road rears
to strike along the slope and spit
its gravel on the ravaged hill that wears
humpback the millstone terraces of spent

and broken village. My mother helplessly
wove her life's poverty in this mill shed.
Her father quarried stone where industry
pillaged the hill, looting its bone to build

a warscape village, the tied house he paid
his health for in the stretching battery
of terraces, the moor's starveling child
straddling its mother's wounded belly

since the hill workings failed. A Chapel
points faith's hope, tickling stone
but missing sky, where men chopping the fell
quarried to shape subsistence prison

and girls at looms wove ignorance to dress
their lives dependence. And the surround
of moor won slow starvation. A relentless
rust at its kissing sabotage unmanned

the iron on the fell. Stealthy terrorists
of wind and frost sapped the mill wall. Here,
beleaguered in its barricade outposts,
the expedition failed. Now the wolf moor

licks at its wounds with tissue greens
grassing to flesh the healing scars
of poor allotments and deserted pens.
The landscape says this stone was never yours.

In tumbled walls, hostage and held for fee,
it knows survival patience and will know
its womb again. It settles now to be
organic with itself, primal where you
were always strangers. This slow ferocity
of grass counter-attacking tells you so.

3.

And afterwards I knew with certainty
that I, on her smooth body had contrived
of purity and lust another geography,
an older contour. Once more I had moved

on maps of my own need. Each broken wall
and dead encampment had its footpaths plain,
was mythic to my route and fundamental
in all my journeys. On her I had drawn

marches of a familiar landscape,
an arid terrain that I knew and when
its features were assembled they would shape
a whole cartography of upland pain.

Team Photographs

1. Team Photographs

George led me to the wall where thirty one
photographs in black and white proposed
thirty one seasons of a side that never won
anything. Young and brash, we colonised
in callow ranks athletically transfixed,
a team without distinction. First, he stared,
not at myself but at Hugh Naylor, relaxed,
arms folded, head erect in an assured
self-confidence in some earlier team.
George spoke, voice loaded with reproach,
'You know the story, that man did me harm.'
He moved to point my later photograph -
'You're sitting where he sat.' - struck visually
to shape our present quarrel. Seasons later, young,
I poised the same null landscape over me,
the slowly vitiating and corroding
townscapes of a time and mood less innocent
than I or our young faces had supposed.
Black and white stripes posed celluloid assent.
Petrified, agonistic, we advertised
different seasons of a side that never won
anything. Upland behind us were
the marches of a landscape I had known,
the blind and narrow town under the moor,
the pattern of the mean, ascending streets
that fashioned us. George pointed Naylor
and myself, wearing corrupting industries,
complicit in that landscape's weather.

2. Some metaphors for the Ground

From a turn in the road, the town lies
camping the moor's flank. Street fingers feel
and grope the fell. Chapel chimneys
tickle its thigh, the jugular canal
arteries through emptied mills. The decayed
white of asbestos stands unleagued
commemorates a side that specialised
in relegation. The pitch preens, grassed
to jewel, in the armpit of this dross
den under the moor. Chapels fail
in bids for re-election: factories
smoke on the transfer list where football
wears faces ripe to move from innocence
in seasons of a side that never won
anything, sliding a limbo dance
from league to league within its worn
tatter of terraces. Folded arms
and fossil grins commemorate a side
- hardened old pros in their last games
and aspirant lads, some of them on the road
to higher leagues - a schizophrenia
matched in results. The white asbestos
leans monument to lost sides that wear
thirty one seasons of a team that tows
its past to swell the grudge offence that sits
the streets and alleyways of this blind
tent under the moor where relegation waits
to stalk us in seasons not yet played.

3. Manager: Arthur Buckley

Manager: Arthur Buckley. It proclaimed
one of lifer's losers. Empty and likeable,
the world's fool, still my friend, unchanged
except his age and girth. He'd stayed the affable
man I remembered. The full-back features,
the swollen, heavy muscles of the neck,
retained their trademark. His body was
fuller but not much clumsier. He took
pride in old photographs damp had spoiled
with emulsions' bombs. Some were past teams,
some, action fragments scissored from old
newspapers, some gripped by blurred frames,
in postures fixing the naivete
that held him gullible, the easy butt
of more worldly games. He could betray
my secret ridicules to grief, a target
making my blame ambiguous for one
of life's persistent losers. *'In this game*
for twenty years, what have I ever won?
No medals. Never a cup.' I pitied him,
not his incompetence or lack of prizes,
but all he never knew, his dull goodness.
His world would need new rules and referees
for him to kiss its cups or wave its trophies.

4. Landlord of The World's End

Our meeting was deliberate enough,
myself and Naylor, near *The World's End*,
his newest strumpet, perching its fief
of moor and car-park. The accident
that scraped his wife to leglesslesss showed
no scratch on his surface. We climbed to
the moorhead. Beneath us, the town splayed
its legs in the offence of streets we knew,
that shaped simplicity within the space
our ignorance permitted. He spoke
derisively -*'An arsehole of a place'*-
turning to gloat his *World's End's* wantonness
slutting the moor. *'It's mine. I always said
I'd have it. Something sodlike crushes'* -
he pointed -*'our sort down there. I made
certain of better.'* Across the moor
his painted excrescence winked. I guessed
that there Agnes might cuddle the lure,
of paper-back romances. Some malice paced
my own derision. *'How's Agnes been?'*
*'She talks about you, Usually that night
dancing with you. She used to carry on.'*
Despair or some once admiration might
have prompted him. He knew what I had tried.
'There's always Alice, can't be wasted.'
His equal irony brushed aside
my own. *'Which of us is the bastard?'*

5. Some sonnet conversations

(i) Alice Buckley at The World's End

I knew the mock refinement of her voice
dismissing me as salesman when she said,
'He isn't here -' squawking her compromise
noises, not remembering me. *'Did
Hughie know you were coming? Are you new?'*
The photograph behind her on the wall
was one I'd seen before. On it the row
of losing faces bubbled on a swell
of town and moor, a team on its way
to winning nothing. *'Mister Naylor's there -'*
she pointed where he sat. *'He used to play
for England when he was a footballer.
He's out today.'* She queened in his affairs
and thought she knew my business. I knew hers.

(ii). Landlord of The Dog

'And so, you're back among us -' On his wall,
the serried photographs were spanning
thirty one seasons of a side that fell
steadily through the leagues. Shorts too long
and heavy boots were ranked in black and white,
shirts luminous under the hill.
He nodded to me. *'Hugh Naylor's got*
The World's End now. Tarted it up to pull
the gin trade.' 'Does he get it?' He laughed.
My thought had been the vacant grey
of car park. *'Gets it alright,'* he said.
'A bit more than he should, I've heard. Let's say,
visitors who might be better off
home with their husbands. Your sort of stuff.'

(iii). George in The Dog

'A different lad then, wasn't he?' George said.
His fingers misted glass to blur
Naylor's young face in a side that stared,
arms folded, heads erect, forever
under fallen landscapes. *'Do you want*
a life like that, one of the bastards?
Hugh Naylor seemed to think they wouldn't
get to him. If you don't play your cards
better, it could be your life in a mess.
I've never had a lot of time for that —
his bloody silly games with Alice -
keep off it. You're sitting where he sat.'
Coincidence of more than cameras was
ground for his theme. He knew my business.

(iv). No stranger to the place

'This was a decent pub until that git -'
he meant Naylor - *'killed it.'* It survived
virgin in his memory, a white
dream his once innocence had pastured.
'There's him and Buckley's tart of a wife -'
'That's an old story.' He turned to avoid
a new and glossier photograph,
Naylor and Buckley, team-mates in a side
screwing towards defeat. The bubble boys
grinned into times not innocent from times
not innocent. *'That git and Buckley's*
floosie -' I thought of Agnes. Other games
flared photographic homilies, chance
ironies well away from innocence.

(v). Agnes Naylor at The World's End

'And as for Alice, couldn't you see
I've known about her playing his queen.
Couldn't you see I knew?' I saw that she
needed to tell me, had always been
ungulled. *'I'm not so foolish. I've known*
about the others.' I looked for spite,
some spring of sourness in her and saw none.
'His little weakness.' Then I knew that
she hadn't been opponent of his games
but agent and entrepreneur and they
were gestures of a sort, her schemes
a kind of love, even compassion.
And then she struck. *'You got your ration.'*

(vi). Landlord of The Dog

On ruined and recorded landscapes, those
apocryphal photographs still wore
in agonistic, schizophrenic rows,
old disillusion or endeavour.
For his own ironies, he pointed
Buckley and Naylor, team-mates in a side
on the way down. *'You know he's resigned
today? Poor bloody Arthur,'* he said.
'A job for Naylor?' Maliciously,
I fed the snippet to him, let him wind
his answer. *'He does one job for Buckley.
Greedy to give him the other.'* And,
outside irony and unaware,
he was still laughing. I'd had my share.

6. A rhetoric for Naylor's penitence

'I've had enough of Agnes. You can't tell
what I've put up with.' Scalding water
that he endured, I found unbearable.
'That whole bloody business with the car -'
He didn't finish or need to finish.
I knew about the car, but better,
its acid preludes. She danced to squash
her sour recriminations in my ear,
resentment fouling the night. Arthur
and Alice Buckley shared the table.
Someone took photographs. Naylor,
quarrelsome, drunk and incapable,
half-killed her on the way home, although
he stayed unscathed. She lost her legs. That was
the business with the car. *'I've had enough,*
it's too much in the end.' In places
penance shower didn't reach, he raised
lather to conceal confessional.
'I want what going but can't get past
Agnes. It's left me with buggerall.
I never wanted more than my ration.
Just some sort of relief and mainly
what you're getting. Alleviation.
My life is skint.' That was his only
occasion of complaint, the one time
I saw the hurt sitting his centre
in loquacious seconds when he came
clean in an assault of scalding water.

7. Those old photographs

'We've had them out. The albums. Old ones -'
Thirteen at table, a white cloth's furl.
a glaze of sharp magnesium hardens
apostle faces. *'Your red-haired girl –'*
Buckley blinks central, haloed by an arch
of window, car headlights on the fell.
His palm lies upward, there is an ash-
tray, wafers and red wine. We smile,
in dresses and suits. Randy Agnes
fixing that flash in virgin white betrays
little except her smirk for Alice
at that strange supper. Her gesture stays.
Naylor leans near Buckley, his pose
mocks innocence. My red-headed girl,
now George's complaint, at that time knows
nothing, though my wafer lust was all
bursting for Agnes. By far the best-
looking, randy and available,
who, when we danced, salacious promised
all that I wanted. Her tongue was full
of spite, jealousy and resentment
tricking her flesh's desire to splay
her readiness for a dance more urgent.
On the drive home, he scraped her legs away,
and that was that, our dancings undone.
All we proposed while smiling behind
the modelled cloth, the wafers and the wine,
the smoking ashtray, never happened.
Captured prophetic, Arthur Buckley
beams innocence where Hugh Naylor
postures the eternal judas-lie.
Alice smiles enigmatic, seems to stare
at truth on or beneath Agnes's dress.
*'We've had them out. Old photographs that shame
you at your games. Touching up Agnes,
and that girl you shagged. What was her name?'*

8. Housewarming

'No holy water with it?' I'd never known
Naylor to water whisky. *'Where's the tap?*
I'm driving.' I recalled he'd driven
drunker. As children, we'd known the shape
of houses like this, were dough in these
unleavened alleys and knew the cage
of their yards, their rooms' geographies.
His water was charade to camouflage
words for my ear. We measured a bare
space of stone-flagged kitchen. *'Buckley's*
finished. I don't know what they've told her.'
Our host's housewarm laughter cut across
his secret. *'If she knows,'* - he eyed the regions
where Alice stood - *'she hasn't said. Cancer.'*
Awed confessional and the kitchen's
cold air penanced it. *'Only a year*
they give him. I hope he never knows.'
Which flesh or whose betrayal he ought
never to know I never knew. The brass
tap spun under his hand. Water spat,
rumbling piped to blur his confession
although he kept his glass well outside
its splutter. *'Some circumstances when*
camouflage matters,' I think he said.

9. Apples for a dying man

'He loves to sit among his apple trees.'
Alice told spreading orchards to cheer
his illness. *'Out in his summer-house.'*
Arthur was watching from his lawn's square
a match of wind and bloom. Six lean trees
were losing badly in an enclosure
of concrete, on that poor pitch, for his
last season's game. Fragile, immature
blossom was being kicked to defeat.
His hair had greyed, his cheeks sunk and thinned,
the bull-neck lost its force. He nodded at
the trees' flimsy bloom. *'If you come round
a bit later, I'll give you some fruit.'*
Wind butting urban sunshine culled
unfruiting seed. Sucking at bottled
stout for his health, he raised his glass to pour
badly, spilling liberal froth that rode
towards the trees. Bottle and flower
conflicted in his mood. *'Guinness is good.
What did I win but relegation?'*
Seen from his shelter, the match had run
to its result. The bitter question
blew from his mouth, like the froth was borne
downwind to join the fallen bloom that,
once promising succulence, now lay
among the dead leaves and the birdshit,
latent to spur a richer life. Maybe.

10. A threnody for dancings done

'It's a long time since we were dancing –'
Agnes cadenced her tentative phrase
towards me, unsure but still causing,
as she had intended to cause,
recall of a time when we had had
hope of a different dancing as we danced.
That night she spent her venom in tirade
condemning Naylor. Now she evidenced
her need that I might still remember
our conspiracy. On the way home,
still angry, he broke the car and her.
It cost her her legs. That quarrelsome
night of our dancing brought back to me
her offers of a more urgent dancing,
recalled her acid mood and finally
her features, finely beautiful, parading
her crudest promises to my ear.
I searched new ironies for a face
once beautiful but now angular,
distorted and that night's ugly voice
the gentlest that I knew. She had been
urgent then, queer lewdness in her tone,
projecting it as her game's design.
And afterwards, as he drove her home,
that cruel, crippling business when
he broke the car and her. My thought hung
on the spaces of her life since then.
'It's a long time since we were dancing –'

11. Blackberry and apple pie

'He can have his home-grown apples with them –'
She poured the berries slowly and they ran
like blood in an enamelled sunstream,
pulsed liquid and uncurdled, from one
bag to another. *'Yes, it's cancer.'*
Thin plastic squealed where her fingers fought.
'Blackberry and apple pie.' Her anger
held all malignant nature in garotte.
She screwed the neck, with deliberation
tightened it, to burst the berries' blood.
Ribbons of juice spurted a profusion
for vicious lubricant to her mood.
'With his own apples '- Jewelled sun lurched
on fruit debauched, bulging as she strained
to scorpion anger where she arched
and stung herself. Under her blenched hand,
swollen and tight, the red membrane burst
to spurt slush fruit. I heard her scream
of anger the distending bag released.
'What use are fucking blackberries to him –'

12. A fireplace with a copper hood

'Tell Naylor I know now.' A tongued fire
was blazing, brawling a copper throat.
His face, reflected, was a skull and wore
a medieval mask of death. A bright
scutter of ash moved firelight within
its indentations. His bitter words
swelled in a metal cheek's emblazon
on moquette. He slid dull eyes towards
team photographs, the lost sides askew
over the hooded fire, where in the line,
himself and Naylor grinned the same spew
of rotting stands. 'What did we ever win?
It's all a bloody cheat.' Firelight was
scraping a face ridged by the moquette's
impress. 'I know that now.' His braces
drooped slack to slip frail shoulders. His
trousers gaped where once his belly had
swollen the waist. A bluster of wind
was sucking elastic tongues renewed
from the flat fire. 'Tell Naylor I found
out in the end.' Which flesh and blood
treacheries he'd solved I never knew.
Such words he howled from that copper hood
were all time's relegations blowing through
poor sides unleagued shaping the bleak
metaphor of narrow streets, the sour
untruths of chapels, the god we make
from images of fear at what we are.

13. Requiem

Thirty one photographs still enshrine
those sides unfutured in their team rows,
screwing to private relegation.
Decaying asbestos stands enclose
the jewel pitch. Mills slouch degenerate
under the moor. Heads erect, arms folded,
agonistic, we commemorate
thirty one seasons of a limbo slide,
thirty one seasons of flesh and blood's
latent treacheries. Buckley's cheer,
if it survives, must simplify sides
in alien leagues. With Naylor,
I share ungrounded fixtures, played
away from home. More than the cameras'
coincidences fix us among greed
mills and chapels where our faces
stare into time not innocent from time
not innocent. We posture the bruised,
legitimate offspring of our noisome
camp on the moor, propose the crude
bible of matches lost in its streets,
acknowledge as our father the god
of games where relegation waits
to stalk us in seasons not yet played.

Seven lost Chapels

1.

She was the moor's merchantman,
a Flying Dutchman riding at harbour
under the fell, anchoring among
rough tugs of terraces. Bumboat graves
crowd with their chandlery.
Captain and crew are ghosts, her galleys
ornate only with whispers, her cargo
now dust, her port a backwater.
She lifts her prow to something
swollen sea-fields of moor, black birded,
that once she towed in her wake,
will never again acknowledge.

2.

I am The Word. Milesian
musclings made me, dynamite
my midwife, crude iron
my nurture, my nature stone.
In the rough trinity
of blast, wrench and grind,
I found myself. Tablets of stone
announce me and whatever
god is immanent in me,
I celebrate in stone.
My covenant is stone.
I am The Word.
The Word is stone.

3.

Ingham's crescendo doctrines
announce his pulpit fulminations.
What will be will be. Never
eat black pudding. Here, under
the witch hill always threatening
a Beltane resurgence, his echo
wrangles back Demdike, Chattox,
the moor's supposed witches, conjuring
evil's alchemic rebirth in
congealing pig-blood. I flesh him
summoning his fear, acknowledging
the black arts' nearby frisson.

4.

Heathcliff, she called me. For years
I was her chapel. We shared the old
rough dialect until they prised
her from me, shifted my fashions and
dressed me gentleman to wear
a softer religion. I have long despised
my new Sunday cloak, their prissy
hymnals staining my casements.
I have endured here, under the moor.
Now she has left them and they bleach me
a ghost. *Heathcliff,* I hear her call.
Soon, I shall be tumbling her again.

5.

Chicken shit rules. Where cockerel
ranters once pulpited salvation's
imminence, clucking congregations
of hens are fouling a cracked font.
Beasts nuzzle at suspended
Stations along shit walls and dung's
malleable religion erects a shining
corridor, a soft statuary of saints.
Such nice conversions
were never the moor's business.
Brackened with ancient heresies, he
leans waiting outside the door.

6.

Out of mortar's manacle, stone
seeks its kind again. The moor
knows its own. Ruin's metaphor
swells the chapel intricacies
of soft diameters of grass,
the juice hypotenuses
of water's leach. Can the caliper
grip wind or gauge the latent
animus of flex and season,
tell mildew's stellar mechanics
and the seed's wrench, the root's slow
hunger, rain's lisping appetite?

7.

Only a boggart methane flares
her deserted Sundays. Ghosts
gather in her dumb pews. Silences
of a pumped harmonium swell
umbilical in her belly.
The soaring, mute acoustics of
remembered rantings hover
her gutted galleries. Wraiths
repent. A shadow preaches dust
to dust. Under the echo-weight
of phantoms, she sinks weekly
a prayer deeper into spoiled earth.

Neighbours

They claimed the moor for neighbour, etched their farms
- *Rake Head, Windy Harbour* - in acid parishes
where vision led. Names gaunt with truth dissenting
the seasons' rituals, crude as wind ranting
its barren testaments. Faith's harbingers, they preached
labour's utilitarian religion.

Trespassed their neighbour's cloisters, sacked his shrines
- *Nut Shaw, Barley Top* - where they commanded
walls built to stem or swerve his sour recoil.
Syllables relevant as famine, each name
the thing it was, security against
the moor's revenges. They staked his land their own.

These were their lime evangelism's chapels
- *Stone Fold, Wet head* - faith's proper prisons,
sites christened by the land's austerity.
With pulpit vowels, hallelujah consonants
denied the moor's religion, raised their psalms
apostate in their neighbour's mysteries.

Bibles of picks and ploughs, they consecrated
- *Old Barn, New Barn* - names nodding at hunger.
From laagered missions, won among the infidel
intake some scattered gestures of conversion.
Nothing recanted. No miracle redeemed
indigenous atheism in the grass.

The bald moor holds them now. The leper stations
- *Cronkie, White Riding* - where vision foundered
stand sepulchres to that dead neighbourhood
gospelled in names. Nobody stayed. No labour
prospered to breach the moor's truth. Nothing appeased
a god dissolved in different sacraments.

Runes

ab tells the moor's thigh,
black boulder muscled,
whose flex is seasons.

eb tells the vault's tears
whose fall from no face
speaks heaven's absence.

ib tells blood whose curdle
at the sun's bandage
grows the bones' wound.

ob tells the moor's eye
whose always staring
forbids the sun's escape.

ub tells flesh whose wound
by the sun's sickle
begets blood's boroughs.

bu tells the moor's thought,
whose substance no substance,
whose icon is wind.

bo tells night's ball, earth's soul,
whose silver scar in void
is skin's lost search.

bi tells day's ball, earth's rod
erect whose muscle plunge
and spurt bays increase.

be tells the bones' hydraulic
palace and prison
whose prism is pain.

ba tells the cipher name
whose wound and sound
unsayable fuels the stars.

Sumwhyle wyth wormez he werrez, and with wolves als,
Sumwhyle wyth wodwos, that woned in the knarrez.

A language for stones

This was a language for rough land.
Within its structures move the residues
of a more brutal world. An older rhetoric
asserts the echo rememberings
of a cruel supernatural.
Hard vowels trap the rituals of blows:
harsh consonants haunt with resonances
of the knapper's hand. Within its rhythms
exist the gestures of the primitive,
asserting fen and fell. Alliteration hauls
a syntax more of moor than meadow,
a grammar of rough transits outside the silk
civilities of assonance and rhyme.
The innate parables of its movement
acknowledge codes and hierarchies
of older and unforgiving gods.

It makes a direct stab into the senses,
a word's sword leaving the page,
its onomatopoeic and alliterative assault
enclosing felt experience
in the first rituals of its making.
This language fights. Is a knarre sharper,
more threatening, harder than rock?
It carries an attachment to the thing
more energetic than aimless naming,
where sound and function are moulded,
propelled into the senses' world.
Faith moves in metaphors of rock:
such transits cannot exist in knarrez.

Long Causeway

1.

The moor's identity hides
in neolithic chambers. Menhirs
jut into air, root enigmatic
in alien lodging. Megaliths
circle, conceal tanged arrowheads.
The high causeway loops, disdaining
the soot valleys' patterns and codes
of cotton's history.

2.

                 Here was harbour
for corpses sailing overnight to burial,
haven territory for the scared wakes
of generations tuned otherwise
to evil's omnipresence. Here lay
landfall safety from the imagined
devilments of the moor, asylum
on consecrated earth.

3.

                 Cash soils.
Landowner avarice and the greed
of putative tenancy bargain to sough
the moor's utility. Coal's tonnage
annexes the grass. Trial borings:
the mineral values of ores: the lie
and dimensions of seams and beds.
Then comes price. Five hundred guineas
for each exploited acre of coal.
The road's census counts custom sold
to capital's manoeuvres.

4.
                              The moor
accepts now the cathedral elegance
of turbines, sweep propellers threshing,
to garner wind, cull air's fertility.

Saltways Catechism

Who names the moor?
  'I,' said the drover.
'In Bastard Clough, through Sod's Toll, at Hard Labour,
christen the salt's power.'

Who psalms the moor?
  'I,' said the curlew.
'At Love Clough, on Tolerance, over Sweet and Mellow,
chant the salt lanes below.'

Who pays the moor?
  'I,' said the drunkard.
'Through Swiggit, round Ale Corner, in Tosspot's Yard,
salt tickles the landlord.'

Who knows the moor?
  'I,' said the pony.
'Up Skidders' Bank, on Whip Hill, down Stumble Valley,
lugging the salt's economy.'

Who clothes the moor?
  'I,' said the grass.
'By Meadow Head, in Horsehold, under Goodshaws,
ripped by the salt's traverse.'

Who cheats the moor?
  'I,' said the shrine.
'At Jesus Wept, at Mary's Chair, across Zion,
concealing salt's religion.'

Who shapes the moor?
  'I,' said the track.
'From Rake Head, over Slate Pits, at High Turnpike,
with salt wounding my back.'

Who sweeps the moor?
    'I,' said the rain.
'Down Foul Syke, down Deep Ditch, down Filthy Drain,
 salt to salt the waters run.'

Who shrives the moor?
    'I,' said the whip.
'From Jericho, round Hades, up Hell's Rip,
speaking salt's ownership.'

Who rules the moor?
    'I,' said money.
'Without me, Famine Ridge, Bleak House, Poverty,
salt worthless, the shrines empty.'

Whitsun

Listen: rearing into hills
the road hymns release
from prison terraces,
promising somewhere else.

It leans a Jacob's ladder
to scale the encroaching moor
where tankers, fonts sour
with acid, clatter under

the fell's scowl. Lorries altared
with quarrying's process rattle
the day's matins, haul
out of shadow, shuttle trade

to further highways.
A changed prospect assembles
another landscape's walls
and different geographies.

Listen: the whining vehicles
of choirs traffic epistles
under the moor's oracles,
promising somewhere else.

Bladdering Whitsun's banners,
infidel wind shudders
the flexible architectures
of Zion where the boxed gears

of hymns grind parables
contesting sceptical contours.
A sermon's engine stutters
the road to Christian bliss.

Prayers broker a faith
alien to the moorhead's
agnosticism. The summit breeds
maps for belief's untruth.

Riding the landscape's quarrel,
the road makes manifest
different distances. Christ
inhabits the wind's swell

of blustering banners where
the tankers' daily religion
corrodes. The land's skin
is scored with acid: the moor

is yearly burned: the fells
daily quarried. The road's census
tells only its traffic's use,
promising nowhere else.

Cracked Mary's Mill

1.

They call me mad. My father's,
his father's father's mill this was.
Now mine. Brick broken fingers
crude for the sky's soft pieces.
I watch through dolly-blue, false
curtain of my window-glass's stain,
cavorting children dance my walls.
Weeds reach to trip. I laugh in noon
green to the sun, stalk ruinous
garden's tangle, my father's
paths, my mother's luminous
borders blown. Convolvulus
is snakes, still parasol cow-
parsley cracks. Elderberries
flutter my hand's rape. Now
among mossed Morrises,
dead Papa's cars, and fungus
Fords, Mama's, I twine green
by the burst walls' bellies.
Was once their mill. Now mine

2.

Copperplate, indentured,
forty apprentice orphans
fevered within a week. Rye bread
so black and soft it clung the gums
like putty, sometimes porridge
sour and blue their foul diet.
Poor starvelings, before that rage
pestilence, death's appetite,
fell at their looms, committed
life on the cloth, were maimed by
senseless machines. Screaming died.
Saw horrid visions. Secretly
at night, my father's father,
his father fired to clean the stall,
pitch and tobacco to deter
the fever's rampage, had girls sprinkle
vinegar to cure the beds
of retching children. So much death,
rumour swears their shallow sheds
unconsecrated heave beneath
Fords and mossed Morrises
of my tumultuous soil.
Some say their bones crack in these
blenched towers of weed, straddle
their flesh through elders, bulge in
fat palms of hut-high nettles
as another century's pain
whose squalor forces the rank grass.

3.

I am the white flower's dance
in the night garden, twisting,
am moth and phosphorescence.
Am maiden silk trysting
with ghosts. Am seven veils bare.
My midnight garden riots
pregnant with phantoms. They are
here, those fevered unfortunates.
Fat worms have awled them. The gleam
belly of lodge butting the weir
quivers old anguish. I am
the cupped convolvulus flower.
In the stilled wheel's genital,
their screaming. My midnights' breed
cold flames in the crumbled wall.
I am the white petal freed.
More than the mousing cats, these
shadows cluster. One of them
loves me. His name is Peerless.
Among mossed Morrises in drum
landscapes we lie. He touches me
strangely. Oh, then the fine
champagnes of my body. Peerless
speaks secretly his passion.
I am my mill's Salome
at midnight nautches where,
damaged and exultant, I
dance the cracked flesh's grandeur.

Barley Top

1.

I wear them, ranting bastards,
my blood forebears, children
of unforgiving creeds,
acid within their moor. Malign

religioned as their weather,
abrasive as their hinterland's
hostility, liming to nurture
a bitter soil. Arthritic minds

raised chapels, rheum endowed
harmoniums groaning a Zion
complicit with their wound,
foetal within their landscape's pain

of names rotted to debris,
their walls' atavism, their intake's
compliant apostasy.
We wear implicit the impress

of maps transmitted through
long generations to compel
blood's shared imbroglio
with the lineaments of our fell.

No logic nominates the ground
or sanctifies the contour's stain.
To understand the wound
is not to heal the pain.

2.

I rant them, catechism,
those garble citadels of the moor,
names conjured in the prism
of a wry religion's grandeur.

Grime, Limers, Bullion:
Myrtle Earth, Rush Candle, Mean Hey:
Jericho, Noah, Zion,
Egypt: Slate Pits, Folly.

I name them, blackened bibles
of intake's apostasy,
assume their gibber syllables
in a rammel psalmody.

Ratten, Feist End, Gibbet:
Nouch, Lench, Gorple, Doal,
White Riding: Old Nick, Boggart:
Wormden, Bleakholt, Bone Hole.

I chant their dearth oblation,
the fossil babels of the fells,
seized in their weather's incantation,
germane within their vowels.

Nut Shaw, Delph Brink, Coppy:
Mary's Chair, Tolerance, Love Clough:
Horsehold, Whittle, White Kink, Cronkie,
Windy Gate, Rake Head, Nab Rough.

I tell their gabble rosary,
blab chapels of that plangent zeal,
intone their plainsong irony,
barren and evangelical.

Famine Ridge, Further, Windy Harbour,
Wreck Beds, Bleak House, Stone Crop:
Slack Myres, Wet Head: Hard Labour,
Needless, Poverty, Barley Top.

3.

Came to the ruined, dry-walled farm
in one of the barren folds of the hill,
its rafters raking the wind, its barn
vanished, but on the spanning lintel, still

crudely but deeply chiselled was the name
I'd sought, the legend, *Barley Top*. It crooned
of my grandfathers' boyhoods, wasted time,
life undernourished on infertile ground.

Even now, though rushes and bog-tufts spread
and vaulted walls and dragged aside the door,
a different, limier green betrayed
land lost by and recaptured by the moor.

I thought of those old builders, the sour land
desolate, unpropitious to their hope.
The name declared an optimism and
sheep they must have kept, but *Barley Top*

spoke languages of pathos, the frail nimbus
of stillborn dream, and *Barley Top* broken,
crumbling at the moor's relentlessness,
was every foundered hope for me then.

Wind trapped and blundering among the stone
took me to times that solitary, wry,
my grandfathers acknowledged as their own,
shoeless before the turning century.

4.

My father's father's feral
apocrypha rolled his father's
mage annexation of the fell.
Sick sheep, the halt ram Topaz

barking in frost, the black mule
Benjamin staggering lame
from winter saltways. His oracle
voices roared millennium.

a benign weather's imminence,
while snow suckled the bacon blots
of his flock's abortions and bones
buckled in rain. The milk goats

drooped shrivel tits. Winter strangled
and wind boiled the grasses
where beltane bracken brindled.
A delivery of voices

pronounced that place's site,
which slab to lay, the solemn grain
of rafters: where communion light
should hole the walls, each stone

a mad *Hallelujah,* every slate
a cracked *Amen.* Deaf hearing learnt
the stars' clattering turn, blind sight
swung angels on his firmament

to garrison sunset, tied tongue
catechised clouds. Another
delivery of voices slung
anarchic bulletins to blather

that place's name. The maul
possessed his chisel and something
arcane within the lintel
compelled his ouija christening

of *Barley Top*. What wry
epistemologies or hopes
conjured that alphabet queerly
occult in his disease?

Lime failed his intake ventures.
Flocks rotted. Halt Topaz died
and the mad currency of voices
crashed on within his head.

No logic nominates that ground
or sanctifies his contour's stain.
To understand the wound
is not to heal the pain.

5.

Greenteeth. They named their horror.
The witch fell's schism
bred him their moor's familiar,
its instinct ectoplasm.

Winter carcasses bared his tooth,
ghost wethers bleated his hymns.
Black birds chanted him. *Greenteeth*
spun inchoate in their names.

His holt was stinking water.
They met his boggart gloss
in methane alleys, his cadaver
loom in the amorphousness

of mist. Scared genets skittered
the echoes haunting gullies
where euphemism slithered
syllables of his alias.

The Irish carving canals
felt him shudder the spade's plunge,
wince at the pick. In candle tunnels
heard the shibboleth revenge

of dialect name their fear.
Semantic in sour soil, he hung
cognate in sounds, his spectre
colloidal in their mouthing.

Greenteeth. In gnostic chapels,
Rechabite roarings congealed
his darker doctrines. Taradiddles
maimed their psalms. Heresy cawed

in anthems. A coven drum
tumped Amen. Hallelujahs spat
carrion to gorge the phantom
hermetic in the pulpit.

6.

I map my father's Uncle,
quarryman, scraping the bone
of moor, who heard the rankle
instinct in its skeleton

and met its spectre mason,
a phantom his memory wrenched
from some diorama frisson
nightly shadowing his bed.

His transoms fractured, his doors'
cartilage buckled, their frames
contorted by the insidious
ratchet of the moor's carapace.

Two names haunted his lodge:
Beelzebub, Ichabod.
Portent in his sortilege
casting of runes foretold

malevolence underground,
a cockatrice, milesian
muscling of stone, earth's wound
opening for the millennium

of Revelation's Six Six Six,
Apocalypse's magma
pulse of the new basilisk
unfossiled, beating Omega.

His jambs skewed. Lintels henged
inimical. The gradient rolled
the moor's frame in a scavenged
shamble to charnel his field.

Stone shocked his door's bastion.
The mole instinct of spoil
gnawed his tilth. He heard *Abaddon*
breathing skulls to his wall.

No logic nominates his ground
or sanctifies his quarry stain.
Geologies of his wound
abjure his map of pain.

7.

I wear him narrow minded,
my father's father, exile
from Barley Top, whose toad
So be it, Lord, whose servile

Amen, I early learned
were fox propitiation
of his Omerta godhead,
whose *Hallelujah* equation

meant Heaven's ambush wrath
averted. Never the squander
barkings of a laudation faith
but gold return for his vendetta

redeemer, one equally engrossed,
his mafia Jehovah,
by acquisition, cash and lust.
The moor's witch anathema

claimed him, stirred apostate,
congealing his litanies,
vital and unregenerate,
usurped the Hebrew pieties

renting his pew. A religion
barren as stone, severe
as hunger fermented his bone.
Barley Top clawed his fervour.

Its Eden anthems hauled him
in the years he blasted stone,
still acolyte of its prism
altar, its bleak persuasion.

Now trucks in crippled phalanxes,
testudo at the ginny's head,
emblem the moor's spent industries,
correlative of the cracked

apocrypha of his faith.
Lost intake strangles the slope.
Wind wrangles the rafter teeth,
unbuilds the walls of *Barley Top*.

8.

Brash in the moor's economy,
their outpost's arcane scrape
scratches a stone. Its irony
mocks their labour. *Barley Top.*

I wear that cipher name,
my witch emblem of the fells
where wind charnels a scheme
of supine stone. The lintel's

menhir mumbles the chisel's
runing, a wryness that honed
my father's father's parables
of hope dissolved in acid ground.

Now bog-cotton and rushes burn
its hearths, bracken panels the door,
lime's fossil taint runs stubborn
in intake garbled by the moor.

The name survives, its pathos
- faith's impotent contour
in the moor's relentlessness -
encodes their leper tenure.

Wind blundering the grass
conjures with bones. I mourn
my father's father, shoeless
under the century's turn.

9.

I chart a ribald pentecost
to map my father. I am
the child beside him, late in frost
allotments, the moon chromium

with cold, the path's steel tempered
to tuning fork, ringing my frisson
footsteps in tensile air. Then seized
on rigid rods, in iron

equipoise, I saw those planet
skulls of chrysanthemums, blight
icon worlds, iced element
of nowhere, their frozen orbit

stemmed higher than my breath
clouding in cold. Moon was
a brittle paleolith.
In that white starlessness,

snow spun a wafer spectrum
of crumbled glass. But nebular
and insensible, that system
burst its void paternoster

to sear my knowing. No faith
survived that existential kiss
of golem otherness, unbirth
of all pathetic fallacies.

Moon leered that orrery,
poising each automaton head
in nowhere's primal nullity.
Till then, no miracle released

the codes of emptiness whose curse,
green in my gut, spoke parable
of nothing's stoic universe,
of being's ishmael babel.

From then, we mortared chapels
in different stone. For him,
the moor's sour canticles,
scrape intake's whining psalm,

the hill's enigma prism,
wore god's undoubted signature.
Two crossed sticks' barbarism
nailed his profoundest rapture.

I map that frost damascus,
still coldly absolute,
my gethsemane dogmas
of the sprit's vacuum transit.

10.

I carve it with words' maul,
that mapping : *Barley Top* : redeem
the page's arcane lintel
with its ouija autism.

I map its prison landscapes,
its prisms of ancestry,
its esemplastic equipoise
in love's commodity.

Barley Top shapes my deity,
unfolds the castrate parables
of intake, the geld psalmody
in rank upland's syllables,

flares boggart and ineffable
in the mind's methane alleys, looms
amorphous in blood's garble
nothing. Its anarchisms

poise the apostate equation
congealed in ruin's metaphor
that spayed us the fell's children,
erotic eunuchs of the moor.

I map myself, bone puppet
of that taint blight whose stigma
revels in flesh's state,
ingrains the witch anathema,

eidetic and embedded in
the landscape's lie: articulate,
ferments in skin's palatinate
internecine, *Barley Top's* stain

usurping the litanies
renting my flesh. I know that mantis
whose numen is to fuse
nothing's barren enigmas.

I carve the icon index
occult within its avatars,
the infibulating paradox
hermetic in our altars.